36

STUDY GUIDE

Conflict and Tension: The First World War, 1894–1918

AQA - GCSE

www.GCSEHistory.com

Published by Clever Lili Limited.

contact@cleverlili.com

First published 2020

ISBN 978-1-913887-35-3

Copyright notice

All rights reserved. No part of this publication may be reproduced in any form or by any means (including photocopying or storing it in any medium by electronic means and whether or not transiently or incidentally to some other use of this publication) with the written permission of the copyright owner. Applications for the copyright owner's written permission should be addressed to the publisher.

Clever Lili has made every effort to contact copyright holders for permission for the use of copyright material. We will be happy, upon notification, to rectify any errors or omissions and include any appropriate rectifications in future editions.

Cover by: Ernest Brooks on Wikimedia Commons

Icons by: flaticon and freepik

Contributors: James George, Jordan Hobbis, Marcus Pailing

Edited by Paul Connolly and Rebecca Parsley

Design by Evgeni Veskov and Will Fox

All rights reserved

DISCOVER MORE OF OUR GCSE HISTORY STUDY GUIDES
GCSEHistory.com and Clever Lili

THE GUIDES ARE EVEN BETTER WITH OUR GCSE/IGCSE HISTORY WEBSITE APP AND MOBILE APP

GCSE History is a text and voice web and mobile app that allows you to easily revise for your GCSE/IGCSE exams wherever you are - it's like having your own personal GCSE history tutor. Whether you're at home or on the bus, GCSE History provides you with thousands of convenient bite-sized facts to help you pass your exams with flying colours. We cover all topics - with more than 120,000 questions - across the Edexcel, AQA and CIE exam boards.

GCSEHistory.com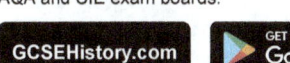

Contents

How to use this book 5
What is this book about? 6
Revision suggestions 8

Timelines
Conflict and Tension, 1894-1918: First World War 12

Overview
First World War 14
Militarism 14
Alliances 15
Imperialism 15
Nationalism 16

The Great Powers of Europe
The Great Powers 16
Britain 17
France 18
Russia 19
Germany 19
Austria-Hungary 20

Rising Tensions
Triple Alliance 21
Triple Entente 21
Arms Race 22
The Naval Race 23
The First Moroccan Crisis, 1905-6 23
The Second Moroccan Crisis, 1911 24
The Bosnian Crisis, 1908-9 25
The First Balkan War, 1912-13 26
The Second Balkan War, 1913 27
Balkan Nationalism (The Black Hand) 27
The Assassination of Archduke Franz Ferdinand 28

The War Begins
The July Crisis, 1914 29
Britain's Entry Into the War 30
The Schlieffen Plan and its Failure 30

Stalemate!
Establishment of the Western Front 31
The Trench System 32
Deadlock on the Western Front 32

The Development of Tactics and Technology
Tactics and their Development 33

Development of Weapons 1: Machine Guns 34
Development of Weapons 2: Aircraft 34
Development of Weapons 3: Poison Gas 35
Development of Weapons 4: Tanks 36
Development of Weapons 5: Artillery 37

Key Battles
The Battle of Verdun, Feb-Dec 1916 37
The Battle of the Somme, July-November 1916 38
The Battle of Passchendaele, July-November 1917 39

War on Other Fronts
The Sinking of the Lusitania, May 1915 40
The Battle of Jutland, May-June 1916 41
Submarine Warfare, 1915-18 42
Anti U-Boat Measures 42
Impact of Naval Blockade on Germany 43
The Gallipoli Campaign 44

The End of the War
Impact of Russian Revolution on German Strategy 45
The Ludendorff Offensive, 1918 45
The Entry of the USA to the First World War 46
General Haig 47
Field Marshall Foch 48
The Hundred Days Offensive, August-November 1918 49
The End of the First World War 50

Glossary 51
Index 53

Quizzes, amazing exam preparation tools and more at GCSEHistory.com

HOW TO USE THIS BOOK

In this study guide, you will see a series of icons, highlighted words and page references. The key below will help you quickly establish what these mean and where to go for more information.

Icons

WHAT questions cover the key events and themes.

WHO questions cover the key people involved.

WHEN questions cover the timings of key events.

WHERE questions cover the locations of key moments.

WHY questions cover the reasons behind key events.

HOW questions take a closer look at the way in which events, situations and trends occur.

IMPORTANCE questions take a closer look at the significance of events, situations, and recurrent trends and themes.

DECISIONS questions take a closer look at choices made at events and situations during this era.

Highlighted words

Abdicate - occasionally, you will see certain words highlighted within an answer. This means that, if you need it, you'll find an explanation of the word or phrase in the glossary which starts on **page 51**.

Page references

Tudor *(p.7)* - occasionally, a certain subject within an answer is covered in more depth on a different page. If you'd like to learn more about it, you can go directly to the page indicated.

WHAT IS THIS BOOK ABOUT?

Conflict and Tension 1894-1914: the First World War is a wider world depth study that investigates international relations. The course focuses on the causes and course of the First World War. It considers how and why the conflict occurred, as well as why it lasted so long.

Purpose
This study will help you to understand the complexities and diverse interests of different states alongside a study in the development of military tactics and technology. The course will enable you to analyse cause and consequence, making links between, and assessing the importance of, events in their historical context. It will also develop your critical evaluation skills.

Enquiries
Conflict and Tension 1894-1918: the First World War is split into 3 key enquiries:
- Enquiry 1 examines the long and short term causes of the First World War.
- Enquiry 2 looks at the development on the Western Front in 1914 and how the nature of trench warfare led to stalemate.
- Finally, enquiry 3 is a study of the reasons why stalemate was finally broken in 1918 and Germany defeated.

Key Individuals
Some of the key individuals studied on this course include:
- Kaiser Wilhelm II.
- Archduke Franz Ferdinand.
- Count Alfred von Schlieffen.
- General Sir Douglas Haig.
- General Erich von Falkenhayn.
- General Erich Ludendorff.
- Field Marshal Ferdinand Foch.

Key Events
Some of the key events and developments you will study on this course include:
- The formation of the alliance system.
- The Anglo-German naval race.
- International crises in the Balkans and Morocco.
- The assassination of Franz Ferdinand.
- The establishment of the Western Front in 1914.
- Key battles on the Western Front: Verdun, the Somme, and Passchendaele.
- The development of new weapons.
- The war at sea.
- The Ludendorff Offensive.
- The Allied 100 days.
- German defeat and the armistice.

Assessment
Conflict and Tension 1894-1918: the First World War is examined on paper 1. You should spend 1 hour on this section of the paper. There will be 4 exam questions which will assess what you have learned from the course.
- Question 1 is worth 4 marks. This question will require you to examine a source, and explain its meaning in its historical context.
- Question 2 is worth 12 marks. This question will require you to examine 2 sources, and assesses your ability to evaluate sources for a particular purpose.
- Question 3 is worth 8 marks. It requires to you to explain and analyse historical events in relation to cause and consequence.

WHAT IS THIS BOOK ABOUT?

- Question 4 is worth 16 marks plus 4 marks for spelling, punctuation and grammar. Here you will be required to make a judgement about the importance of an event or development in an extended response.

REVISION SUGGESTIONS

Revision! A dreaded word. Everyone knows it's coming, everyone knows how much it helps with your exam performance, and everyone struggles to get started! We know you want to do the best you can in your GCSEs, but schools aren't always clear on the best way to revise. This can leave students wondering:

- ✓ How should I plan my revision time?
- ✓ How can I beat procrastination?
- ✓ What methods should I use? Flash cards? Re-reading my notes? Highlighting?

Luckily, you no longer need to guess at the answers. Education researchers have looked at all the available revision studies, and the jury is in. They've come up with some key pointers on the best ways to revise, as well as some thoughts on popular revision methods that aren't so helpful. The next few pages will help you understand what we know about the best revision methods.

How can I beat procrastination?

This is an age-old question, and it applies to adults as well! Have a look at our top three tips below.

◎ Reward yourself

When we think a task we have to do is going to be boring, hard or uncomfortable, we often put if off and do something more 'fun' instead. But we often don't really enjoy the 'fun' activity because we feel guilty about avoiding what we should be doing. Instead, get your work done and promise yourself a reward after you complete it. Whatever treat you choose will seem all the sweeter, and you'll feel proud for doing something you found difficult. Just do it!

◎ Just do it!

We tend to procrastinate when we think the task we have to do is going to be difficult or dull. The funny thing is, the most uncomfortable part is usually making ourselves sit down and start it in the first place. Once you begin, it's usually not nearly as bad as you anticipated.

◎ Pomodoro technique

The pomodoro technique helps you trick your brain by telling it you only have to focus for a short time. Set a timer for 20 minutes and focus that whole period on your revision. Turn off your phone, clear your desk, and work. At the end of the 20 minutes, you get to take a break for five. Then, do another 20 minutes. You'll usually find your rhythm and it becomes easier to carry on because it's only for a short, defined chunk of time.

Spaced practice

We tend to arrange our revision into big blocks. For example, you might tell yourself: "This week I'll do all my revision for the Cold War, then next week I'll do the Medicine Through Time unit."

REVISION SUGGESTIONS

This is called **massed practice**, because all revision for a single topic is done as one big mass.

But there's a better way! Try **spaced practice** instead. Instead of putting all revision sessions for one topic into a single block, space them out. See the example below for how it works.

This means planning ahead, rather than leaving revision to the last minute - but the evidence strongly suggests it's worth it. You'll remember much more from your revision if you use **spaced practice** rather than organising it into big blocks. Whichever method you choose, though, remember to reward yourself with breaks.

Spaced practice (more effective):

week 1	week 2	week 3	week 4
Topic 1	Topic 1	Topic 1	Topic 1
Topic 2	Topic 2	Topic 2	Topic 2
Topic 3	Topic 3	Topic 3	Topic 3
Topic 4	Topic 4	Topic 4	Topic 4

Massed practice (less effective)

week 1	week 2	week 3	week 4
Topic 1	Topic 2	Topic 3	Topic 4

REVISION SUGGESTIONS

What methods should I use to revise?

Self-testing/flash cards

Self explanation/mind-mapping

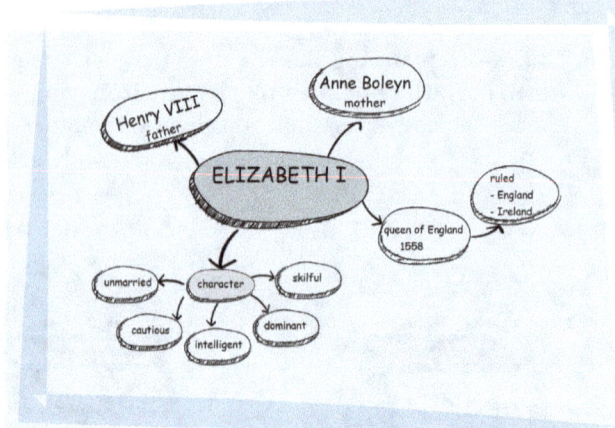

The research shows a clear winner for revision methods - **self-testing**. A good way to do this is with flash cards. Flash cards are really useful for helping you recall short – but important – pieces of information, like names and dates.

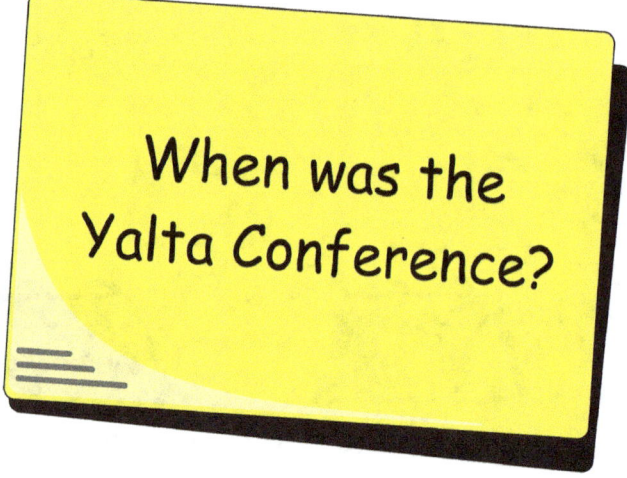

Side A - question

Side B - answer

Write questions on one side of the cards, and the answers on the back. This makes answering the questions and then testing yourself easy. Put all the cards you get right in a pile to one side, and only repeat the test with the ones you got wrong - this will force you to work on your weaker areas.

pile with right answers

pile with wrong answers

As this book has a quiz question structure itself, you can use it for this technique.

Another good revision method is **self-explanation**. This is where you explain how and why one piece of information from your course linked with another piece.

This can be done with mind-maps, where you draw the links and then write explanations for how they connect. For example, President Truman is connected with anti-communism because of the Truman Doctrine.

Quizzes, amazing exam preparation tools and more at GCSEHistory.com

REVISION SUGGESTIONS

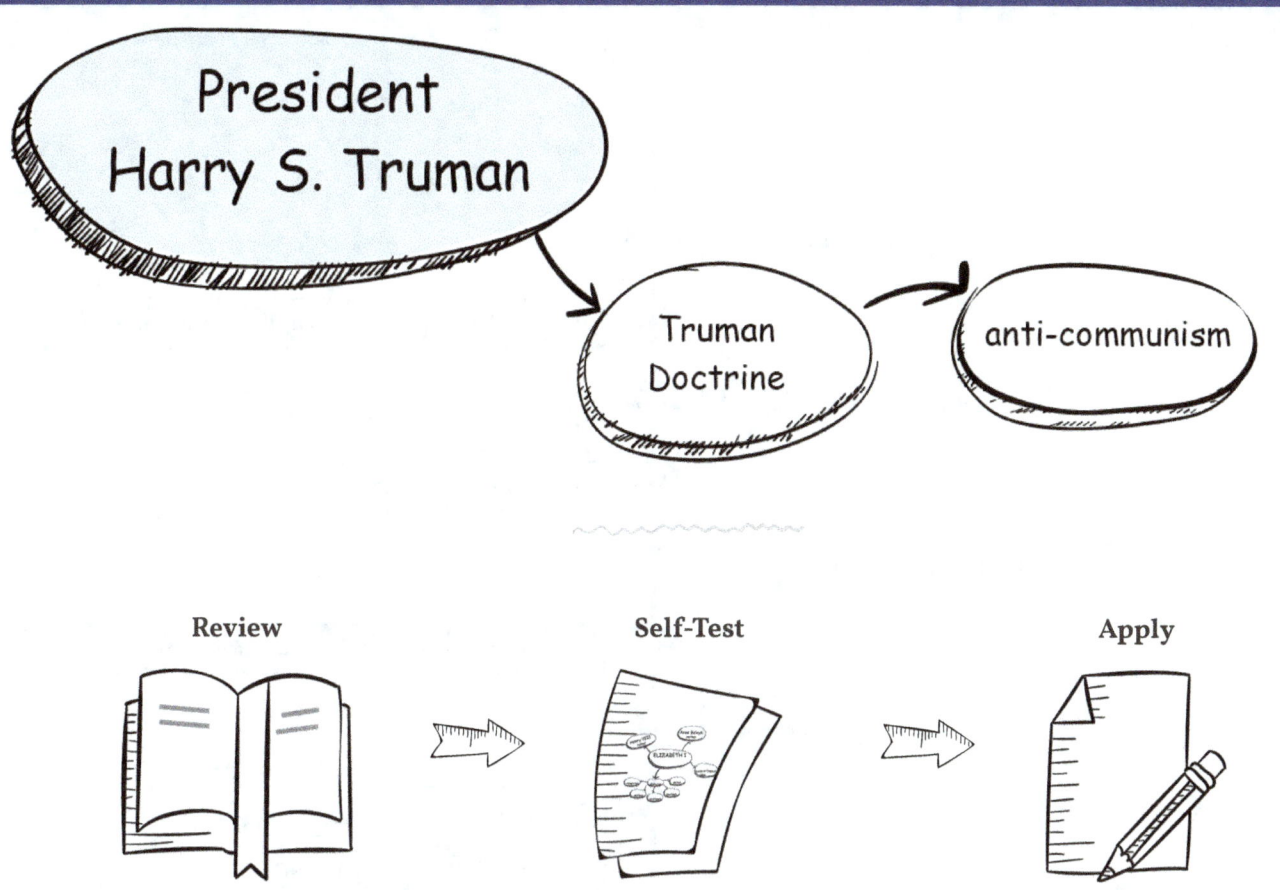

Start by highlighting or re-reading to create your flashcards for self-testing.

Test yourself with flash cards. Make mind maps to explain the concepts.

Apply your knowledge on practice exam questions.

Which revision techniques should I be cautious about?

Highlighting and **re-reading** are not necessarily bad strategies - but the research does say they're less effective than flash cards and mind-maps.

Highlighting

Re-reading

If you do use these methods, make sure they are **the first step to creating flash cards**. Really engage with the material as you go, rather than switching to autopilot.

CONFLICT AND TENSION, 1894-1918: FIRST WORLD WAR

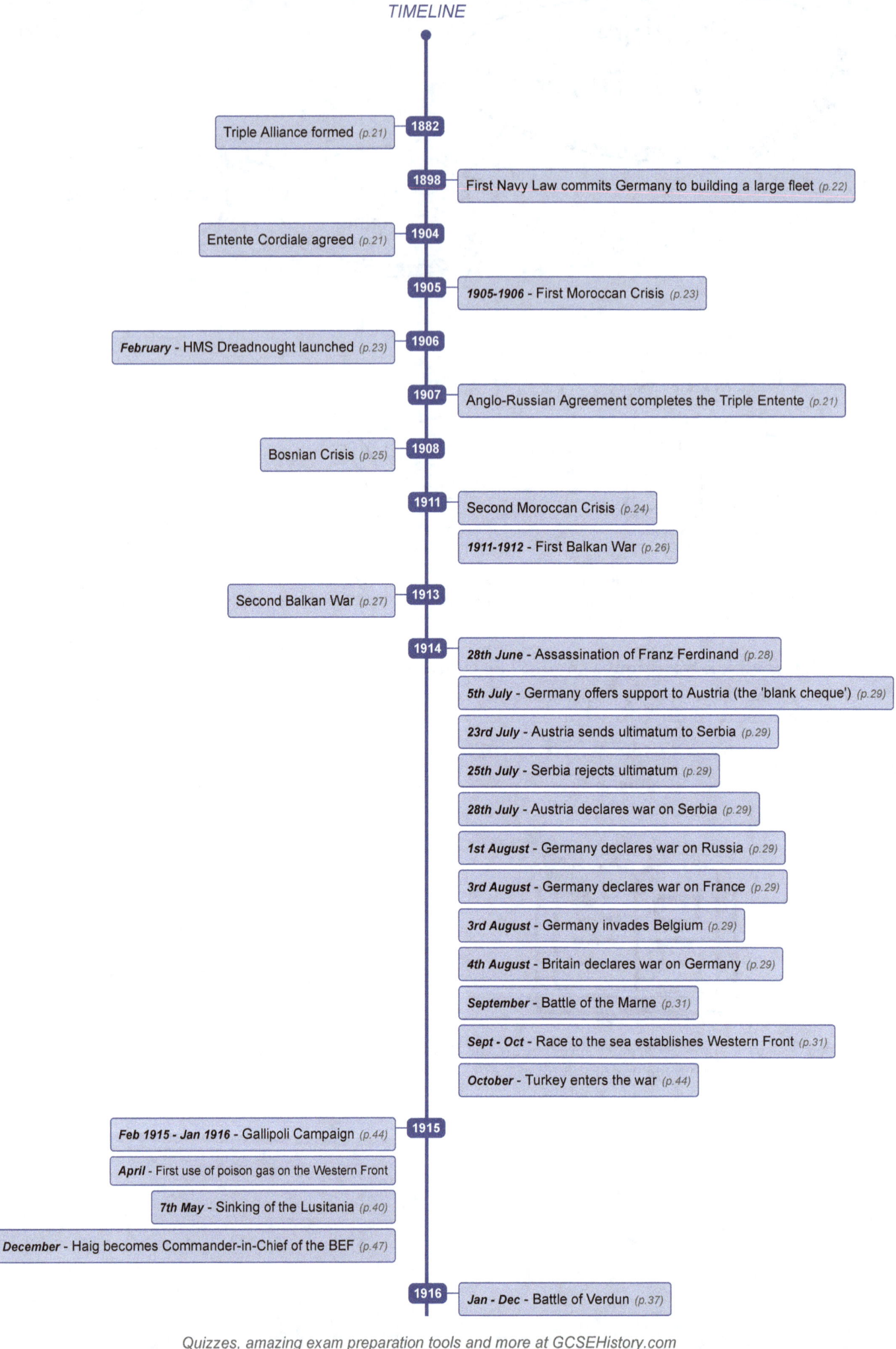

TIMELINE

1882 — Triple Alliance formed *(p.21)*

1898 — First Navy Law commits Germany to building a large fleet *(p.22)*

1904 — Entente Cordiale agreed *(p.21)*

1905 — *1905-1906* - First Moroccan Crisis *(p.23)*

1906 — *February* - HMS Dreadnought launched *(p.23)*

1907 — Anglo-Russian Agreement completes the Triple Entente *(p.21)*

1908 — Bosnian Crisis *(p.25)*

1911 — Second Moroccan Crisis *(p.24)*
1911-1912 - First Balkan War *(p.26)*

1913 — Second Balkan War *(p.27)*

1914
- *28th June* - Assassination of Franz Ferdinand *(p.28)*
- *5th July* - Germany offers support to Austria (the 'blank cheque') *(p.29)*
- *23rd July* - Austria sends ultimatum to Serbia *(p.29)*
- *25th July* - Serbia rejects ultimatum *(p.29)*
- *28th July* - Austria declares war on Serbia *(p.29)*
- *1st August* - Germany declares war on Russia *(p.29)*
- *3rd August* - Germany declares war on France *(p.29)*
- *3rd August* - Germany invades Belgium *(p.29)*
- *4th August* - Britain declares war on Germany *(p.29)*
- *September* - Battle of the Marne *(p.31)*
- *Sept - Oct* - Race to the sea establishes Western Front *(p.31)*
- *October* - Turkey enters the war *(p.44)*

1915
- *Feb 1915 - Jan 1916* - Gallipoli Campaign *(p.44)*
- *April* - First use of poison gas on the Western Front
- *7th May* - Sinking of the Lusitania *(p.40)*
- *December* - Haig becomes Commander-in-Chief of the BEF *(p.47)*

1916 — *Jan - Dec* - Battle of Verdun *(p.37)*

CONFLICT AND TENSION, 1894-1918: FIRST WORLD WAR

- *31st May - 1st June* - Battle of Jutland *(p.41)*
- *1st July - 21st Nov* - Battle of the Somme *(p.38)*
- *August* - Creeping barrage tactic begins to be used *(p.37)*
- *September* - First use of tanks *(p.36)*
- *Winter 1916-1917* - 'Turnip winter' in Germany *(p.43)*

1917

- *January* - Zimmerman Telegram sent *(p.47)*
- *1st Feb* - Germany resumes unrestricted U-boat warfare *(p.42)*
- *2nd April* - USA declares war on Germany *(p.46)*
- *July - Sept* - Battle of Passchendaele *(p.39)*
- *October* - Russian Revolution *(p.45)*
- *November* - Successful massed tank attack at Battle of Cambrai *(p.36)*

1918

- *March* - Foch becomes Commander-in-Chief of all Allied forces on the Western Front *(p.48)*
- *March* - Russia signs peace treaty with Germany *(p.45)*
- *March - July* - Ludendorff Offensive *(p.45)*
- *8th Aug - 11th Nov* - Allied 100 Days Offensive *(p.49)*
- *October* - German navy mutinies *(p.43)*
- *9th Nov* - Kaiser Wilhelm II abdicates *(p.50)*
- *11th Nov* - Armistice signed *(p.50)*

FIRST WORLD WAR

The First World War was the largest and most widespread conflict in history up to that point

What was the First World War?
The First World War (also known as the Great War) was a global conflict that lasted from 1914-1918.

Who was on each side in the First World War?
The war was fought between the Central Powers (Germany, Austria-Hungary, Bulgaria, and the Ottoman Empire) and the Allied Powers (France, Russia, Belgium, Serbia, and Britain). The Allies were later joined by the USA and Italy.

When did the First World War take place?
The First World War started on July 28th 1914, and ended on 11th November 1918.

Where did the First World War happen?
The First World War took place across the world, both on land and at sea. Most of the fighting occurred in Europe and Russia, although there were smaller battles in the Middle East, Africa and China.

Why did the First World War happen?
The war broke out due to a number of short and long term reasons, which can be summarised as follows:
- Militarism *(p.14)*.
- Alliances.
- Imperialism. *(p.15)*
- Nationalism *(p.16)*.
- Economic rivalry.

DID YOU KNOW?

Use this mnemonic to help remember the MAIN causes of the war:
- Militarism
- Alliances
- Imperialism
- Nationalism

MILITARISM

Strong armed forces were important to maintain Great Power status

What is militarism?
Militarism is the idea that a country should have a strong military and be prepared to use it.

How did militarism lead to the First World War?

Due to the alliance system, countries grew afraid of being surrounded by hostile states. As a consequence, they increased the size of their armies and navies, which created more fear and led to an arms race.

> **DID YOU KNOW?**
>
> Alfred Vagts, a German historian, defined militarism as 'the domination of the military man over the civilian, an undue preponderance of military demands, an emphasis on military considerations.'

ALLIANCES
Alliances were used to balance power in Europe

 What were the alliances in the First World War?

There were two pre-First World War alliances. The Triple Entente *(p.21)* consisted of Britain, Russia and France. The Triple Alliance *(p.21)* was formed by Germany, Austria-Hungary and Italy.

 How did alliances lead to the First World War?

In order to achieve security, countries often formed alliances to protect themselves. Tensions between alliances meant that, when Austria-Hungary declared war on Serbia in 1914, others felt obligated to join the conflict.

> **DID YOU KNOW?**
>
> **Family loyalties were soon tested!**
> George V (England) and Wilhelm II (Germany) were actually first cousins! However, the family ties didn't stop there. George and Tsar Nicholas II were also first cousins and joined forces in the Triple Entente.

IMPERIALISM
The Great Powers were keen to protect their empires

 What is imperialism?

Imperialism is the desire to acquire colonies and create an empire.

 How did imperialism lead to the First World War?

Germany attempted to challenge the large overseas empires already held by France and Britain. This was an issue as colonies provided raw materials, and were markets for goods produced by the European powers that governed them. If they lost these, they lost money.

Who were the countries which followed a policy of imperialism?

The European powers and their overseas colonies in 1914 were as follows:

- ☑ Great Britain had 56 colonies, with a total population of 390 million.
- ☑ France had 29 colonies, with a total population of 58 million.
- ☑ Russia had 0 colonies, although it was looking to expand in the Balkans.
- ☑ Germany had 10 colonies, with a total population of 15 million.
- ☑ Austria-Hungary had 0 colonies, although it did control other European countries such as Bosnia.

> **DID YOU KNOW?**
>
> In the Los Angeles Times on 20th July, 2003, Edward W Said wrote: "Every empire, however, tells itself and the world that it is unlike all other empires, that its mission is not to plunder and control but to educate and liberate.'

NATIONALISM

Most Europeans felt a strong sense of pride in their countries

What is nationalism?

Nationalism is having strong support for your own country's independence and interests. This may lead to people believing their country is superior to others.

How did nationalism lead to the First World War?

When nationalism is too strong, it can lead to competition between countries. This inspired many people to support war and join up to fight in 1914. This is closely linked to imperialism *(p.15)* as it promotes the idea of one 'superior' country ruling over others.

> **DID YOU KNOW?**
>
> It was an intensified form of nationalism that led to the outbreak of the First World War, though the assassination of Archduke Franz Ferdinand in Sarajevo in June 1914.

THE GREAT POWERS

The most powerful of all countries

What were the Great Powers?

The Great Powers were the most powerful countries in Europe in the years before the First World War. Their competing foreign policies increased tensions between them which ultimately led to the outbreak of war in 1914.

Who were the Great Powers?

There were 5 Great Powers in 1914:

- ☑ Great Britain.
- ☑ Germany.
- ☑ France.
- ☑ Austria-Hungary.
- ☑ Russia.

What were the characteristics of a Great Power?

To be a great power in 1914 a country had to meet the following criteria:

- ☑ Be able to influence and control international affairs.
- ☑ Possess great economic strength.
- ☑ Possess great military power.
- ☑ Possess a stable and competent government.
- ☑ Rule over a large population of people.
- ☑ Control a large empire that possesses lots of resources.

Which countries were not considered Great Powers but were considered second-rate powers?

There were 4 second-rate powers in 1914:

- ☑ Italy.
- ☑ The Ottoman Empire.
- ☑ Japan.
- ☑ The USA.

> **DID YOU KNOW?**
>
> In 1814 diplomats officially recognised the five Great Powers: France, Britain, Russia, Austria (Austria-Hungary in 1867–1918), and Prussia (the German Empire in 1871).

BRITAIN
The British bulldog

What was Britain like in 1914?

In 1914 Britain was the wealthiest country in the world. However, its dominance was under threat from other industrialising countries.

What was British foreign policy in 1914?

Britain's foreign policy had experienced significant change by 1914:

- ☑ In the late nineteenth century, Britain had avoided getting involved in European affairs through its policy of 'splendid isolation'.
- ☑ In the early 1900s, Britain abandoned this 'splendid isolation' due to the growing threat from Germany.

- ✅ Britain became part of the Triple Entente *(p.21)* by 1907.
- ✅ Imperialism *(p.15)* was strong in Britain. It possessed the world's most powerful navy and largest merchant fleet.
- ✅ Britain wanted a balance of power in Europe and always put the defence of the empire first.

 ### What was the British economy like in 1914?

By the start of the twentieth century, Britain was the wealthiest country in the world.
- ✅ London was the centre of global finance.
- ✅ Much of this wealth came from the empire, which was the largest in the world in 1914.
- ✅ However, the economy was in decline as Germany and the USA were overtaking Britain in areas such as coal and iron production.

> **DID YOU KNOW?**
>
> **The British bulldog was soon accompanied by a lion!**
> Its strength, tenacity and willingness to fight larger animals appealed to 18th century political cartoonists, who began depicting the female figure of Britannia accompanied by both a lion and a bulldog.

FRANCE
The French cockerel

What was France like in 1914?

France was economically strong in 1914 and had the second-largest empire in the world, with many trade links.

 ### What was the foreign policy of France in 1914?

Much of French foreign policy centred on the threat from Germany:
- ✅ France wanted revenge on Germany for her defeat in the Franco-Prussian war of 1870, and to regain the rich provinces of Alsace and Lorraine that had been lost after the war.
- ✅ France, therefore, signed military alliances with Russia and Britain to protect herself from German attack.
- ✅ Militarism *(p.14)* was important in France as she underwent large scale rearmament before 1914 *(p.22)* to rival Germany.

 ### What was the French economy like in 1914?

France was an industrialised nation by 1914:
- ✅ It had well developed industries.
- ✅ It was a leader in science and technology.
- ✅ It possessed a large agricultural sector.

> **DID YOU KNOW?**
>
> The cockerel is the symbol of the French people due to a play on words around the Latin 'gallus' meaning Gaul and 'gallus' meaning coq, or rooster.

RUSSIA
The Russian bear

What was Russia like in 1914?
Russia was the largest Great Power, but also the most backward. Its economy was mainly agricultural and its armed forces were poorly equipped.

What was Russia's foreign policy in 1914?
Russia had 2 main foreign policies in 1914.
- It feared the growing strength of Germany, so made alliances with France and Britain.
- As fellow Slavs, Russia supported the Serbs in their struggle against Austria-Hungary in the Balkans.

What was Russia's influence in the Balkans in 1914?
Russia had suffered an embarrassing defeat against Japan in 1905, which weakened Russian influence in the Balkans.

> **DID YOU KNOW?**
> The bear isn't an official symbol of Russia and never has been. Today, the double-headed eagle - as depicted on Russia's national emblem - is the country's official symbol.

GERMANY
The German eagle

What was Germany like in 1914?
By 1914 Germany had the second biggest industrial capacity in the world (after the USA). It had a small empire compared to the other Great Powers.

What was German foreign policy in 1914?
There were 3 main aspects to German foreign policy before 1914:
- Germany feared encirclement by Russia and France so formed the Triple Alliance *(p.21)* in 1882 and increased the size of its army.
- Kaiser Wilhelm II believed that Germany should have its 'place in the sun' - a large overseas empire befitting its Great Power status. This was called weltpolitik (world policy) and required the building of a large navy.
- Formed in 1871, Germany upset the balance of power in Europe by defeating France in the Franco-Prussian War of 1870-71 and creating a rivalry with Russia and Britain.

Who was the leader of Germany in 1914?
The German head of state was a kaiser (emperor). From 1888 this was Kaiser Wilhelm II. He was:
- An erratic ruler, impulsive and prone to outbursts of rage.
- An autocrat. Although he was meant to rule alongside his appointed government he often ignored advice from his government ministers.
- A cousin of King George V and Tsar Nicholas II.

- ✅ Plagued by feelings of inadequacy when Germany was matched against larger empires. This contributed to his decision to go to war in 1914.

What was the German empire like in 1914?

Germany had a small empire compared to the other Great Powers. However, the kaiser had pursued an empire-building policy, which had brought Germany into conflict with Britain and France.

> **DID YOU KNOW?**
> The Reichsadler (Imperial Eagle) is derived from the Roman eagle standard used by the Holy Roman Emperors and in Germany's modern coats of arms, including those of the Second German Empire (1871–1918).

AUSTRIA-HUNGARY
The Austrian black eagle

What was Austria like in 1914?

Austria-Hungary was the weakest of the Great Powers after Russia, with a large but poorly equipped army.

What was the Austro-Hungarian Empire like before 1914?

Austria-Hungary had a European empire containing many ethnic groups and languages, many of whom wanted independence.

What affected Austro-Hungarian foreign policy before 1914?

There were 2 main influences on Austria-Hungary's foreign policy:

- ✅ Domestic nationalism *(p.16)* and racism were powerful forces in Austria-Hungary that created constant tensions with Serbia and Russia over the Balkans.
- ✅ The rise of a newly independent Serbia, supported by Russia, was considered a great threat to the integrity of the Austrian-Hungarian Empire.

What was the foreign policy of Austria before the First World War?

Austria-Hungarian foreign policy had 3 main aims:

- ✅ To limit the power of the newly independent Serbia because it was encouraging the Slavic people of the empire to push for independence.
- ✅ To keep its fragmenting empire together.
- ✅ To increase its influence in the Balkans and therefore, limit Serbian and Russian influence in the region.

What was the Emperor of the Austrian government like in 1914?

Franz Josef I was out of touch with the modern world, and obsessed with reasserting Austrian power in the Balkans at all costs.

What was the Austrian military like in 1914?

The Austro-Hungarian army was large, but outdated and poorly equipped.

> **DID YOU KNOW?**
> The double-headed eagle of the ruling House of Habsburg-Lorraine was used by the Imperial and Royal institutions of Austria and Hungary's dual monarchies.

TRIPLE ALLIANCE
A central European alliance

What was the Triple Alliance?
The Triple Alliance was an agreement between Germany, Austria-Hungary and Italy, to provide military support to each other.

When was the Triple Alliance created?
The Triple Alliance was formed in May 1882.

Who was in the Triple Alliance?
The Triple Alliance consisted of three of Europe's great powers in 1914: Germany, Austria-Hungary and Italy.

Why was the Triple Alliance formed?
The Triple Alliance provided mutual support for the smaller countries; it was a chance to have a more powerful ally. For Germany, the alliance provided protection against encirclement by France and Russia.

> **DID YOU KNOW?**
> The Triple Alliance was originally called the Dual Alliance when it was agreed in 1879. It became the Triple Alliance when Italy joined in 1882.

TRIPLE ENTENTE
Friendly agreements

What was the Triple Entente?
The Triple Entente was a military coalition between the Great Britain, France and Russia against any potential enemies.

When was the Triple Entente created?
The Triple Entente was created in 1907 when Russia joined Britain, who had previously united in the Entente Cordiale in 1904.

Who were members of the Triple Entente?
The Triple Entente consisted of three of Europe's great powers in 1914 - Russia, France and Great Britain.

Why was the Triple Entente formed?
The purpose of the Triple Entente was to protect its members against the growing threat of Germany and to support each other if there was a war.

> **DID YOU KNOW?**
> The Triple Entente was not a military alliance but part of a series of informal agreements. It did not oblige any of the countries involved to defend each other.

ARMS RACE
Preparations for war began years before 1914

What was rearmament like before 1914?
As a result of increasing tensions, from 1900 all the Great Powers of Europe began increasing the sizes of their armed forces.

How much had Germany rearmed by 1914?
Germany had an army of almost two million men at the outbreak of war. It was the best trained and equipped in Europe. Germany had also increased the size of its navy in a naval race *(p.23)* with Great Britain.

How much had Britain rearmed by 1914?
In 1914 Britain had a small, well equipped and well-trained volunteer army of around 150,000 men (the BEF). However, it had the biggest navy by far, beating Germany in a naval arms race in the years before the war.

How much had France rearmed by 1914?
France had a well equipped army of 1.3 million men. It had devised Plan 17 to attack Germany through Alsace-Lorraine if war occurred.

How much had Russia rearmed by 1914?
Russia had a large army of 1.4 million and hundreds of thousands of reserves. However, it consisted mostly of peasants who were poorly trained and very badly equipped.

How much had Austria-Hungary rearmed by 1914?
By the start of the war Austria-Hungary had a poorly equipped army of almost half a million men. It needed the military support of its larger ally, Germany.

> **DID YOU KNOW?**
> A naval build-up highlighted the arms race of the First World War; countries stockpiled huge arsenals of weapons to outdo their opponents.

THE NAVAL RACE
Britain looked to continue its domination of the seas

What was the naval race?
The naval race was a competition between Germany and Britain to have naval supremacy. The race was 'run' between 1906 and 1914.

Why did Germany want to challenge the British navy and start the naval race?
Britain relied on its navy to keep sea routes open to its empire and protect its economic interests. Germany wanted to become a world power, and Britain saw this as a threat to its own empire.

What ships were the focus of the naval race?
In 1906 Britain launched a new battleship, HMS Dreadnought. It was the most advanced warship of the time: faster, more heavily armoured and with bigger guns than previous warships. Germany built its own dreadnoughts, which led to a naval arms race between the two countries.

Who won the naval race?
Between 1906 and 1914 Britain built 29 dreadnoughts, compared with Germany's 17.

DID YOU KNOW?

The Germans didn't have much confidence in their older ships.
During the naval race, Germans called their older ships 'fünf Minuten' because the vessels wouldn't last five minutes against a dreadnought.

THE FIRST MOROCCAN CRISIS, 1905-6
The crisis can be viewed as the beginning of pre-war tensions

What was the First Moroccan Crisis?
The First Moroccan Crisis was a political dispute between France and Germany, after France declared its intention to have control (a mandate) over Morocco.

Which countries were involved in the First Moroccan Crisis?
France and Germany were the main countries involved. France had agreed with other European powers that it would take control of Morocco, but Germany hadn't been consulted.

Where was the First Moroccan Crisis?
The crisis was over Morocco, one of the few independent African states not colonised by a European power.

When was the First Moroccan Crisis?
The dispute took place from March 1905, and was solved with the Algeciras Conference in April 1906.

Why did the First Moroccan Crisis happen?

The crisis emerged due to the Kaiser's desire to promote Germany's strength as part of his weltpolitik strategy, and to test the Entente Cordiale.

 What was the German reaction to the First Moroccan Crisis?

When Germany heard about France's plan to control Morocco, Kaiser Wilhelm II visited Tangier in Morocco to show his support for Morocco's independence. He didn't want France to become too powerful.

 What was the French reaction to the First Moroccan Crisis?

France was shocked by Germany's position. The French press and politicians reacted angrily, as they believed it was a simple matter and Germany should not interfere, given the country's limited number of colonies.

 What were the consequences of the First Moroccan Crisis?

There were 3 outcomes from the First Moroccan Crisis:

- ✓ The crisis was solved with the Algeciras Conference of 1906. It was decided that France would have control over Moroccan affairs, but all countries were free to trade with Morocco.
- ✓ It strengthened the Entente Cordiale and led to the Anglo-Russian Agreement of 1907, therefore completing the Triple Entente *(p.21)*.
- ✓ It angered the German Kaiser greatly. He felt embarrassed, and would not back down in any further dispute. This attitude would eventually lead to the Second Moroccan Crisis *(p.24)*.

DID YOU KNOW?

Kaiser Wilhelm II was furious following the First Moroccan Crisis and demanded revenge.

He exclaimed, 'Paris must get one in the eye from us one day!'

THE SECOND MOROCCAN CRISIS, 1911

This crisis further increased tensions between Germany and the entente

 What was the Second Moroccan Crisis?

The Second Moroccan Crisis was a political dispute between France and Germany, when Morocco appealed for help from France and Spain after rebels rose against the sultan.

 Which countries were involved in the Second Moroccan Crisis?

France, Germany and Spain were the main countries involved. France and Spain both sent troops to Fez in May 1911 to help support the sultan. In response, Germany sent a gunboat, SMS Panther, to the port of Agadir.

 Where was the Second Moroccan Crisis?

The crisis was focused on Fez, a city in the north of Morocco, but it also stretched to the port of Agadir where the Germans sent their gunboat.

When was the Second Moroccan Crisis?
The dispute began in March 1911 and was resolved with the Treaty of Fez in November 1911.

How did Germany react to the Second Moroccan Crisis?
When Germany heard about France's involvement, they believed the French were using this as a way to occupy Morocco. Germany sent a warship to Morocco, as France's actions went against the Treaty of Algeciras.

How did France react to the Second Moroccan Crisis?
The French reacted to Germany's warship by sending more troops to Morocco. Britain tried to persuade France against doing this, but concern about the behaviour of Germany meant they had to support the action.

How did the Second Moroccan Crisis end?
It ended as Germany was hit by a financial crisis and couldn't deal with both events at the same time. The Germans withdrew their warship and left Morocco.

What were the consequences of the Second Moroccan Crisis?
There were 5 key outcomes from the Second Moroccan Crisis:
- The Treaty of Fez was signed between France and Germany, which agreed that France could take control of Morocco. In return, the French would give parts of the Congo to Germany.
- Tensions between France, Britain and Germany reached breaking point. This event showed the lengths all countries would go to in order to defend their interests.
- British support for France during the crisis strengthened the Entente Cordiale.
- The division between the Entente powers and Germany continued to increase.
- It weakened the Triple Alliance *(p.21)*, as Italy did not support Germany in the crisis.

> **DID YOU KNOW?**
>
> **Tensions were already beginning to flare in 1911!**
>
> David Lloyd George issued a warning to Germany to offer fair terms to France, stating that 'peace at that price (British disadvantage) would be a humiliation intolerable for a great country like ours to endure.'

THE BOSNIAN CRISIS, 1908-9
Austria's interest in the Balkans stirred up trouble

What was the Bosnian Crisis?
While the 1908 Turkish Revolution was taking place, Austria annexed Bosnia and Herzegovina, which had been under Turkish control. However, the king of Serbia claimed Bosnia & Herzegovina should belong to his country.

What were the consequences of the Bosnian Crisis?
There were 5 main outcomes from the Bosnian Crisis:
- It increased tension between the alliances, as Russia stepped in to support Serbia, while Germany took Austria-Hungary's side.

- The Balkan League, consisting of Bulgaria, Greece, Montenegro and Serbia, was set up with the goal of forcing Turkey out of Europe.
- Russia backed down and began to rearm.
- Austria-Hungary now felt it could rely on support from Germany in the future.
- It weakened the Triple Alliance *(p.21)*, as Italy refused to support Austria-Hungary.

> **DID YOU KNOW?**
>
> **There was a cover-up attempt by Austria-Hungary to justify its actions in Bosnia.**
> Known as the Agram Trial, Austria-Hungary sentenced 31 Serbs for their role in trying to overthrow the state. However, it was later found that one of the Austrian-Hungarian ministers had forged the documents. The 31 Serbs were then released.

THE FIRST BALKAN WAR, 1912-13
Trouble in the Balkans (part 1)

What was the First Balkan War?
The First Balkan War was a war between Turkey and the Balkan League.

When was the First Balkan War?
The war took place from October 1912 to May 1913.

What countries were involved in the First Balkan War?
Turkey fought against the four members of the Balkan League - Bulgaria, Greece, Montenegro and Serbia.

What happened in the First Balkan War?
The Turkish were overpowered by the Balkan forces, and surrendered after just 50 days of actual fighting.

What were the consequences of the First Balkan War?
Turkey gave up its land in Europe and this was divided between the Balkan states.

> **DID YOU KNOW?**
>
> **Turkey was known as the 'sick man of Europe' at this time!**
> This was due to the decline of the once-feared Ottoman Empire.

THE SECOND BALKAN WAR, 1913
Trouble in the Balkans (part 2)

What was the Second Balkan War?
The Second Balkan War was fought between Bulgaria, Serbia and Greece. Serbia and Greece supported each other and were backed by Turkey and Romania.

What caused the Second Balkan War?
Bulgaria was not happy with the way in which Turkey's land had been divided up among the Balkan League countries.

When was the Second Balkan War?
The war started in June 1913, a month after the original peace agreement from the first war. Bulgaria was soon overpowered, and an armistice was signed in August 1913.

What countries were involved in the Second Balkan War?
Bulgaria fought against Greece, Serbia, Turkey and Romania.

What happened in the Second Balkan War?
Bulgaria invaded Greece and Serbia in June. However, Bulgaria did not expect the unified response from the other countries and was forced to ask for an armistice.

What were the consequences of the Second Balkan War?
There were 5 key outcomes from the Second Balkan War:
- Serbia gained territory and grew more aggressive towards other Balkan countries following its success.
- Serbians in Bosnia-Herzegovina were inspired by the victory and wanted to join Serbia.
- Austria-Hungary became concerned by the possibility of revolt within its empire, specifically in Bosnia.
- Austria-Hungary was committed to trying to control Serbia.
- Bulgaria was resentful of Serbia's gain and was waiting for an opportunity to gain back some of its lost land.

> **DID YOU KNOW?**
>
> **People began to consider and research the impact of war on civilian populations.**
> The Carnegie Endowment for International Peace produced one of the first internationally read reports on civilians during war.

BALKAN NATIONALISM (THE BLACK HAND)
Many Serbians wanted to unite all Slavs

What was the Black Hand?
The Black Hand was a secret society which aimed to unite all Serbs who were ruled by either the Ottoman Empire or Austria-Hungary.

Who was involved in the Black Hand?
The Black Hand was founded by ten Serbian army officers, led by Colonel Dragutin Dimitrijević. However, membership soon grew to more than 2,500 members.

When did the Black Hand form?
The Black Hand was formed on 22nd May, 1911.

Why was the Black Hand formed?
Slavic nationalism *(p.16)* had grown following the Bosnian crisis *(p.25)*, and there was now a desire to unite all Slavs in a Greater Serbia.

What methods did the Black Hand use?
The Black Hand planted bombs, and carried out assassinations and general acts of sabotage in foreign countries which controlled a Serbian population.

Why was the Black Hand important?
The Black Hand would later assassinate Archduke Franz Ferdinand *(p.28)*, heir to the Austrian throne, and spark the beginning of the First World War.

> **DID YOU KNOW?**
> The kingdom of Yugoslavia was formed on 1st December, 1918. The name was created by combining the Slavic words 'jug' (south) and 'slaveni' (Slavs).

THE ASSASSINATION OF ARCHDUKE FRANZ FERDINAND
Death in Sarajevo

What happened to Archduke Franz Ferdinand?
Archduke Franz Ferdinand, the heir to the Austro-Hungarian throne, was shot and fatally wounded.

Who killed Archduke Franz Ferdinand?
Gavrilo Princip, a member of the Black Hand *(p.27)*, assassinated the archduke using a revolver.

Where was Archduke Franz Ferdinand assassinated?
Archduke Franz Ferdinand was assassinated in Sarajevo, the capital of Bosnia.

When was the assassination of Archduke Franz Ferdinand?
The assassination was carried out on 28th June, 1914.

Why was Archduke Franz Ferdinand assassinated?
Archduke Franz Ferdinand was assassinated by the Black Hand *(p.27)* in an attempt to make sure he didn't pacify the Serbians in Bosnia. Pacifying the Serbians in Bosnia would strengthen the archduke's position when he came to

the throne but would also undermine Serbia's plans to unite all Slavs in a Greater Serbia - the Black Hand wanted an independent Serbia, free from Austro-Hungarian and Ottoman rule.

 What were the consequences of the assassination of Archduke Franz Ferdinand?

The main outcome of the assassination was the outbreak of the First World War. This happened in the aftermath of the assassination, during the 'July Days'.

> **DID YOU KNOW?**
>
> Gavrilo Princip, the assassin, was too young to receive the death sentence. He died of tuberculosis while in prison, in 1918.

THE JULY CRISIS, 1914
The assassination led to a 'domino effect' as countries joined the war

 What were the 'July Days' before the outbreak of the First World War?

The July Days is the name given to the period between the assassination of Archduke Franz Ferdinand *(p.28)* and the start of the First World War.

 What were the key events of the First World War 'July Days'?

The July Days are made up of 10 key exchanges between alliances;

- ☑ 28th June, 1914: Assassination of Franz Ferdinand.
- ☑ 5th July, 1914: Germany agreed to support Austria-Hungary in a potential conflict with Serbia. This is known as the 'blank cheque'.
- ☑ 23rd July, 1914: Austria-Hungary sent an ultimatum to Serbia.
- ☑ 25th July, 1914: Serbia agreed to all of Austria's demands except one.
- ☑ 26th July, 1914: Russia promised to support Serbia in any conflict.
- ☑ 28th July, 1914: Austria-Hungary declared war on Serbia. Serbia requested the support of Russia.
- ☑ 29th July, 1914: Germany warned Russia not to get involved but Russia mobilised its army. Two days later, Germany also warned France not to intervene.
- ☑ 1st August, 1914: Germany declared war on Russia and, in return, France mobilised its army.
- ☑ 2nd August, 1914: Germany requested access to Belgium, to attack France as part of the Schlieffen Plan *(p.30)*. Belgium refused. A day later, Germany declared war on France and invaded Belgium.
- ☑ 4th August, 1914: Britain declared war on Germany.

> **DID YOU KNOW?**
>
> During the July Crisis, the Kaiser bizarrely steamed off on his yacht for a Baltic cruise.

BRITAIN'S ENTRY INTO THE WAR
Publicly, Britain joined the war over a 'scrap of paper'

What made Britain enter the First World War?
When Germany invaded Belgium on 3rd August 1914 as part of the Schlieffen Plan *(p.30)*, Britain gave Germany an ultimatum to leave. Germany ignored it and Britain declared war.

When did Britain join the First World War?
Great Britain declared war on Germany on 4th August 1914.

Why did Britain join the First World War?
There were 3 main reasons for Britain joining the war:

- Britain had promised to defend Belgium in the 1839 Treaty of London. Kaiser Wilhelm II called it a 'scrap of paper' and did not believe Britain would honour it.
- Britain could not risk Germany gaining control of ports on the English Channel. This would threaten Britain's overseas trade and empire.
- If Germany won the war, it would dominate Europe and become unbeatable. This would also threaten Britain's empire.

DID YOU KNOW?

The original soldiers in the British Expeditionary Force, or BEF - the six-division British Army sent to the Western Front during the First World War - were nicknamed the 'Old Contemptibles'.

This is because Kaiser Wilhelm though the British had a 'contemptible little army' in 1914.

THE SCHLIEFFEN PLAN AND ITS FAILURE
The Germans had one, inflexible, plan of attack in the west and it quickly began to go wrong

What was the Schlieffen Plan?
The Schlieffen Plan was a German war plan to avoid a war on two fronts by attacking France, travelling at high speed through Belgium. After defeating France, the German Army would then east turn and attack Russia.

When was the Schlieffen Plan created?
The plan was created in December 1905, though it was not employed until August 1914.

Who created the Schlieffen Plan?
The Schlieffen Plan was created by the most senior general in the German Army, Count Alfred von Schlieffen.

Why was the Schlieffen Plan created?
The plan was created in preparation for war due to growing rivalries at the time. Germany was particularly worried about being encircled by France and Russia.

Why did the Schlieffen Plan fail?

The Schlieffen Plan failed for 6 key reasons:

- ☑ The Germans could not keep to the 6-week timetable for defeating France: the Belgian Army slowed the German advance at forts around Liege, while the BEF slowed it further at the Battle of Mons.
- ☑ The use of Plan 17, which was the French war plan to attack Germany's industrial centre, slowed the German advance by two weeks. However, the plan proved an overall failure for the French.
- ☑ Russian mobilisation came more quickly than expected and Russia invaded eastern Germany on 19th August. This caused Germany to send 100,000 troops to the east, weakening its attack against France.
- ☑ German supplies of food and ammunition could not keep up with the rapid advance, leaving soldiers tired, hungry and under-equipped.
- ☑ General von Kluck changed the plan. Instead of encircling Paris he decided to meet the French and British head on and aim to win a decisive victory at the Battle of the Marne, but was defeated.
- ☑ At the Battle of the Marne the Germans were forced back to the River Aisne where they began to dig trenches.

What were the consequences of the failure of the Schlieffen Plan?

The failure of the Schlieffen Plan had 2 important consequences:

- ☑ It meant the Germans would now have to fight a war on two fronts, reducing their chance of victory.
- ☑ The Germans dug trenches to defend their captured territory. This led to the establishment of the Western Front *(p.31)* and stalemate there until the summer of 1918.

DID YOU KNOW?

The Schlieffen Plan was later revised by Colonel-General Helmuth von Moltke the Younger, the Commander-in-Chief of the German Army after Schlieffen retired in 1906.

ESTABLISHMENT OF THE WESTERN FRONT
The Race to the Sea

What was the Western Front?

The Western Front was a system of trenches and fortifications. It was where the Germans fought the French, British, and later, American troops, throughout the war.

Where was the Western Front?

The Western Front ran for over 400 miles from the Belgian coast to near the Swiss border.

Why did the Western Front develop?

The Western Front developed in 3 stages:

- ☑ After the failure of the Schlieffen Plan *(p.30)*, German troops began to dig trenches to protect themselves and hold the territory they had already captured.
- ☑ From September 1914, both sides moved north trying to outflank (get behind) each other. Both sides dug trenches for protection. By November they had reached the coast and could go no further; this is known as the 'race to the sea'.
- ☑ From this point both sides began improving their trenches and strengthening their defences. This was the beginning of stalemate on the Western Front.

> **DID YOU KNOW?**
>
> The Race to the Sea was known in French as 'Course à la mer'. In German it was 'Wettlauf zum Meer', and in Dutch, 'Race naar de Zee'.

THE TRENCH SYSTEM
Trench systems became quite sophisticated

What was the trench system?

Both sides dug networks of trenches to hold their positions on the Western Front *(p.31)*. As they were developed they became more sophisticated, and became the soldiers' homes as well as where they fought.

What were the key features of the trench system?

The trenches had 7 key features.

- Frontline trench. This was the first line of defence, and soldiers attacked from here.
- Support trench. This had support troops, and was also a place to retreat to if the front line was attacked and over-run.
- Reserve trench. This was sited 100m behind the support trench. Troops could rest here when they were not on the front line.
- Dugouts. These were holes, dug into the sides of trenches, where men could sleep or take cover.
- Communication trenches. These were used to connect the other trenches together.
- Trenches were cut in a zigzag pattern to stop bullets travelling a long way down them during an attack, or to stop explosions from travelling along the whole trench.
- No man's land. This was the space between the front lines of each side's trenches.

> **DID YOU KNOW?**
>
> Trenches varied in quality. In some areas they were deep, well drained and well protected, while in others they were just a series of connected shell holes.

DEADLOCK ON THE WESTERN FRONT
Tactics and ineffective weapons led to a lack of progress for much of the war

What was deadlock (stalemate) on the Western Front?

The Western Front deadlock, or stalemate, was when both sides dug into their trenches from which they launched repeated attacks, resulting in very little gain and high numbers of casualties.

Why was there a deadlock on the Western Front?

There was deadlock on the Western Front due to a number of factors:

- The failure of the Schlieffen Plan (p.30). As the Germans failed to advance, they dug in at places which were difficult to attack.
- The strength of defences. Trenches were difficult to attack, especially as barbed wire and machine guns were used in defence.
- Ineffective weapons. Attacking weapons struggled against the strong defences early in the war, although weapons developed as the war progressed.
- The conditions. The geography of the Western Front (p.31) made it difficult to fight. It was difficult to move across ground churned up by shellfire, or turned into muddy quagmires by heavy rain.
- No new tactics. Generals lacked experience in modern, industrialised war. They used old tactics such as cavalry charges and hand-to-hand fighting.

> **DID YOU KNOW?**
>
> One of the biggest myths about the First World War was that most soldiers who were deployed died.
>
> Only 11.5% of those deployed died. As a British soldier, you were more likely to die during the Crimean War.

TACTICS AND THEIR DEVELOPMENT

Tactics had improved by 1918

What were First World War tactics like?

Early in the war most large attacks followed a similar pattern. After a long artillery bombardment to weaken enemy defences, troops would go 'over the top' of their trenches to capture and hold enemy trenches.

What was the purpose of First World War tactics?

For most of the war, tactics on the Western Front (p.31) were mainly concerned with breaking through enemy trenches and ending the stalemate, or killing as many enemy troops as possible in a war of attrition.

Why did First World War tactics fail to break the stalemate?

Tactics were poor and attacks failed for 3 reasons:

- The use of reconnaissance aircraft (p.34) and the preliminary artillery bombardment gave the enemy warning of an imminent attack, and time to prepare.
- Attacking troops crossing no-man's land were exposed to machine gun (p.34) and shell fire.
- The artillery bombardment was ineffective at cutting barbed wire and destroying deep dug-outs.

How did First World War tactics improve?

By 1918 tactics had been improved in 3 main ways:

- Artillery bombardments were shorter and more intense to maintain the element of surprise.
- Infantry advanced under the protection of 'creeping barrages', aircraft (p.34) and tanks.
- Objectives were smaller and easier to defend when captured.

> **DID YOU KNOW?**
>
> Despite the First World War's reputation as a senseless bloodbath whose military operations were devoid of intelligent thought, the period from 1914-1918 was history's single largest revolution in military tactics and technologies.

DEVELOPMENT OF WEAPONS 1: MACHINE GUNS

Machine guns were key to defence

What was the role of machine guns in the First World War?
Machine guns were used to defend trenches throughout the war. A fairly new weapon, they could fire 400-600 bullets per minute with a range of up to 2,000 metres.

What were machine guns like in 1914?
The Germans had 12,000 in 1914, although the British did not use them in large numbers until 1915. They required a crew of four to six operators so they were more suited to defence than attack. They could rapidly overheat or jam.

How did machine guns improve during the war?
By 1918 they were widely used by all armies. The rate of fire had vastly increased and some handheld 'light machine guns' had been developed e.g. the Lewis gun, so could be used by attacking troops.

What impact did machine guns have?
They were one of the key defensive weapons of the war: devastatingly effective against infantry, they could cut down hundreds of advancing soldiers in minutes. However, they prolonged the stalemate rather than breaking it.

> **DID YOU KNOW?**
>
> **Some things stand the test of time...**
> The British Vickers machine gun was still being used by some armies as late as the 1960s.

DEVELOPMENT OF WEAPONS 2: AIRCRAFT

Aircraft developed rapidly during the war

What was the role of aircraft in the First World War?
Aircraft were mostly used to gather intelligence on the enemy. This could be in the form of monitoring troop movements, trench layout or supply chains.

What were aircraft like in 1914?

In 1914 aeroplanes were extremely primitive, unarmed, unreliable and highly dangerous 'string bags'. Losses were very high, especially among new pilots.

How did aircraft improve during the war?

By 1918 aircraft were more specialised:

- ☑ 'Fighters' such as the Sopwith Camel were developed. These, were fitted with machine guns and were much faster and more maneuverable. Dogfights were common.
- ☑ 'Bombers', such as the German Gotha and the British Handley Page, had been designed that could carry heavy loads of bombs and drop them on distant targets.
- ☑ By 1918, 10,000 planes were being used and over 50,000 airmen had been killed.

What were dogfights in the First World War?

As aircraft were fitted with machine guns, they could fire on the men in the trenches and also against other enemy planes, in what became known as dogfights. These were spectacular aerial battles relying on a pilot's skill and reflexes.

What impact did aircraft have?

The war sped up the development of aircraft technology so they became a key weapon on the Western Front (p.31). Air power was also used at sea to observe and attack shipping.

> **DID YOU KNOW?**
>
> **A pilot who shot down five or more enemy aircraft was called an 'ace'.**
>
> The most successful ace of the First World War was Manfred von Richthofen, also known as the Red Baron. He shot down 80 allied planes before being shot down and killed himself in 1918.

DEVELOPMENT OF WEAPONS 3: POISON GAS

Gas was a weapon of terror

What was the role of poison gas in the First World War?

The role of gas was to try and help soldiers break into enemy trenches. Gas would cause terror or incapacitate the enemy. It was released from canisters into no-mans-land.

What was poison gas like in 1914?

Poison gas was not used in 1914 but introduced during the battles of 1915:

- ☑ Chlorine gas was first used by the Germans at the Second Battle of Ypres in 1915.
- ☑ It was released into no-man's land from special canisters hidden in the front line.
- ☑ Thousands of French and Canadian soldiers suffocated or fled in terror from the choking green cloud.
- ☑ In revenge the British used chlorine gas at the Battle of Loos in September 1915. But winds blew the gas back into the British trenches, gassing more of the attacking troops than the Germans.
- ☑ During 1915, all sides began using phosgene and chlorine gas which suffocated and blinded soldiers.

How did poison gas improve during the war?
There were 3 key developments for poison gas during the war:
- ✓ By 1917, more lethal gases were developed e.g. mustard gas which burned the skin and lungs.
- ✓ Gas shells were introduced and fired at enemy lines to overcome earlier problems of wind direction.
- ✓ Specialised gas masks and protective clothing were developed for soldiers, dogs, horses and pigeons, all of whom served in the front lines and were at risk of gas attack.

What impact did poison gas have?
Gas was more of a psychological weapon and did not have a large impact on breaking the stalemate. Gas casualties made up only a small percentage of total casualties as scientists developed effective gas masks. Only 3,000 British troops were killed by gas.

> **DID YOU KNOW?**
> The poem 'Dulce et Decorum est' by Wilfred Owen describes a chlorine gas attack.
> CHALLENGE: Read the poem and see if you can understand why gas was a terror weapon.

DEVELOPMENT OF WEAPONS 4: TANKS
'Lumbering slowly towards us came three huge mechanical monsters such as we had never seen before.' - Bert Chaney, 1916

What was the role of tanks in the First World War?
Tanks were used to cross difficult ground, destroy machine guns, provide cover for advancing infantry and crush barbed wire in front of enemy trenches. They allowed for quick advancement through the enemy trenches and beyond.

What were tanks like in 1914?
Tanks were used for the first time by the British at the Battle of the Somme *(p.38)* in 1916. They moved at walking pace, were not very manoeuvrable and were extremely unreliable - more than half broke down before they got to the German trenches. The Germans did not use tanks until 1918.

How did tanks improve during the war?
In November 1917 at Cambrai over 400 tanks were used and achieved great success. Unfortunately, they blasted through enemy lines so quickly that the infantry could not keep up.

What impact did tanks have?
Tanks were a key weapon in helping to break the stalemate. They were effective when used in great numbers, something that was only possible in the last year of the war.

> **DID YOU KNOW?**
> Tanks were originally called 'landships'. To keep the idea secret the British pretended they were mobile water tanks. The name 'tank' stuck.

DEVELOPMENT OF WEAPONS 5: ARTILLERY
Artillery was the weapon of the Western Front

What was the role of artillery in the First World War?
Artillery was used to bombard the enemy lines by firing huge shells (up to 108 kilograms) in preparation for an infantry attack. The aim was to destroy the barbed wire and the front line trenches which protected the wider trench system.

What was artillery like in 1914?
In 1914 artillery use faced many challenges:
- In 1914 artillery was not very accurate & difficult to 'range' targets by spotting where the shells landed. There was no way for infantry to effectively communicate with the 'gunners' (artillery) from the front line.
- Firing from well behind their own lines, artillery sometimes bombarded their own forward trenches because they could not see where their shells landed.
- By 1915 as many as 50% of British shells were 'duds'.
- Factories could not produce enough shells. The British fired 250,000 shells at the Battle of Loos in 1915 but they called off the attack partly because of a shortage of artillery shells.

How did artillery improve during the war?
From 1915 major improvements took place in the use of artillery:
- Shells improved in quality and quantity meaning many fewer 'duds'; in 1916 'fuse 106' was developed by the British, which was far more effective at cutting barbed wire.
- Howitzers were improved and more widely used. These fired shells high in the air and so could drop shells into trenches accurately, even if they could not be seen by the gunners.
- New tactics had been introduced e.g. the creeping barrage and the box barrage.
- Spotter aircraft *(p.34)*, spotter balloons and radio were being used to send live information to the artillery about where and what to fire at.

What impact did artillery have?
Artillery bombardments caused more casualties than any other weapon. It was a key weapon of the war.

> **DID YOU KNOW?**
> The biggest artillery gun of the war could fire shells weighing over 100kg a distance of 80 miles!

THE BATTLE OF VERDUN, FEB-DEC 1916
They shall not pass!

What was the Battle of Verdun?
The Battle of Verdun was a major battle between French and German forces on the Western Front *(p.31)*.

What happened at the Battle of Verdun?
The main events of the battle were:

- ✅ The Germans attacked and initially made good progress, capturing the forts around the town.
- ✅ French soldiers counterattacked and pushed the Germans back. After several months the German attacks petered out.

When was the Battle of Verdun?
The Battle of Verdun was the longest battle of the First World War, lasting from the 21st January 1916 until the 18th December 1916.

Where was the Battle of Verdun?
The Battle of Verdun was fought in a salient around the French town of Verdun. This was chosen as it was of symbolic importance to the French, and the Germans knew the French would fight hard to defend it.

Why did the Germans attack at the Battle of Verdun?
General Erich von Falkenhayn wanted to 'bleed France white'. The aim was to kill more French soldiers than German, causing the French army to collapse. This is known as a war of attrition.

What were the consequences of the Battle of Verdun?
The Battle of Verdun had 2 main results;
- ✅ Both the French and German armies were weakened.
- ✅ Verdun was saved.

Why did the German attack at the Battle of Verdun fail?
The Battle of Verdun is seen as a German failure for 3 key reasons;
- ✅ The German plan of attrition had failed as they had almost as many casualties (350,000) as the French (400,000).
- ✅ The French appointed General Petain to defend the city. He told the French troops that the Germans 'shall not pass' and ordered the pouring of men and equipment into the Verdun salient along 'the Sacred Way'.
- ✅ In July, the Allies launched their own offensives: the British at the Somme *(p.38)* and the Russians on the Eastern Front. This meant Germany had to pull troops out of Verdun to defend other areas.

> **DID YOU KNOW?**
> Today there is a huge ossuary (grave) at Verdun. Through the windows you can view the bones of over 130,000 French and German soldiers.

THE BATTLE OF THE SOMME, JULY-NOVEMBER 1916
The battle was an Anglo-French effort to break the stalemate

What was the Battle of the Somme?
The Battle of the Somme was fought by British and French forces against the Germans. It was part of an offensive to force the Germans back and achieve victory on the Western Front *(p.31)*.

When was the Battle of the Somme?
The battle took place from 1st July, 1916 to 18th November, 1916.

Where was the Battle of the Somme?
It took place on the River Somme in France, where the British and French armies met.

Why was the Somme Offensive launched?
It was part of an offensive to force the Germans back and achieve victory on the Western Front *(p.31)*. It was also launched to help relieve pressure on the French, who were under attack at Verdun *(p.37)* to the south.

What were the consequences of the Battle of the Somme?
The battle had 4 key outcomes;
- On the first day of the battle there were up to 57,000 British casualties compared with the Germans' 8,000. Haig *(p.47)* continued the attack and, by November, casualties numbered 620,000 for the Allies and 450,000 for the Germans.
- At most, the Allies advanced by 15km along just part of the Western Front *(p.31)*. The expected breakthrough never occurred.
- However, the Germans called off their attacks at Verdun *(p.37)*, saving the French army there.
- The Allies developed new technology (the tank *(p.36)*) and tactics (the creeping barrage), which contributed to victory later.

Why was the Battle of the Somme unsuccessful?
The battle is seen as an Allied failure for 3 main reasons:
- The Germans knew the attack was coming due to aerial reconnaissance. They moved away from the front line into strengthened trenches, some as deep as 12 metres.
- In the week before the attack, 1.73 million shells were fired at the German lines. However, they were not effective in destroying German dugouts or cutting the barbed wire. Additionally, over a third of those shells fired were 'duds' and failed to explode.
- Following the bombardment of shells, General Haig *(p.47)* told soldiers to advance slowly towards the enemy trenches. He believed they would be undefended; but they were not, and heavy casualties occurred.

> **DID YOU KNOW?**
> **The Western Front is still deadly today!**
> Farmers continue to dig up some of the estimated 300 million unexploded shells. This is known as the 'iron harvest'. On average, 3 people die each year from coming into contact with unexploded shells.

THE BATTLE OF PASSCHENDAELE, JULY-NOVEMBER 1917
The battle can be summed up as 'mud and blood'

What was the Battle of Passchendaele?
The Battle of Passchendaele was a joint British and Canadian offensive against the Germans, led by General Haig *(p.47)*.

When was the Battle of Passchendaele?
The battle began in July 1917 and finished on 10th November 1917.

Where was the Battle of Passchendaele?
The battle took place in Passchendaele in the Ypres Salient.

What were the aims of the Battle of Passchendaele?
Haig *(p.47)* wanted to break through German lines and control the coast. He wanted to capture naval bases to make it harder for the Germans to carry out submarine attacks on British ships.

What were the results of the Battle of Passchendaele?
There were 3 key outcomes from the battle:
- After three months of fighting, Passchendaele was captured and Haig *(p.47)* could claim victory.
- The battle came at a cost. A total of 240,000 British and 220,000 German soldiers were wounded or killed.
- In total, the Allies captured around 8km of territory, and Haig *(p.47)* failed to achieve his main objective.

Why did the Battle of the Passchendaele fail?
There were 2 main reasons why the battle plan failed:
- As with the Somme *(p.38)*, the Germans were aware of the coming attack.
- Heavy rains turned the battlefield into a quagmire. Soldiers were knee-deep in liquid mud, making it difficult to move.

DID YOU KNOW?

In the first part of the battle, 19 mines were detonated under the German lines. One crater still exists today - filled with water, it is called the 'Pool of Peace'.

THE SINKING OF THE LUSITANIA, MAY 1915
The sinking caused Germany to change its approach

What happened to the Lusitania?
The Lusitania was a British civilian cruise liner that was sunk by a German U-boat.

When was the Lusitania sunk?
The attack took place on 7th May, 1915.

How was the Lusitania sunk?
The Lusitania departed New York, bound for Liverpool. However, it was torpedoed just 13km from the coast of Ireland by the U20, a German U-boat. The ship sank within 18 minutes.

Who was on the Lusitania?
There were 1,959 passengers on board. Of the 1,198 who drowned, 128 were American.

Why did the Germans sink the Lusitania?

The Germans attacked the Lusitania as there were war materials on board. This made sinking the ship justifiable in the context of war.

What were the reactions to the sinking of the Lusitania?

There was international outrage at the sinking. Britain and America protested and there were calls for America to declare war on Germany. America issued a warning to Germany but did not declare war at that time.

> **DID YOU KNOW?**
>
> After the war, divers confirmed the Lusitania was carrying munitions.

THE BATTLE OF JUTLAND, MAY–JUNE 1916

The war at sea repeated the stalemate of the Western Front

What was the Battle of Jutland?

The Battle of Jutland was the largest naval battle of the First World War, between Britain and Germany off the coast of Denmark.

What happened during the Battle of Jutland?

The Germans intended to draw out the British fleet and make a surprise attack. However, the British already knew of the plan and had sent its fleet ready to attack 259 warships, with 100,000 men on board, fought at Jutland.

When was the Battle of Jutland?

The battle took place between 31st May and 1st June 1916.

What were the results of the Battle of Jutland?

The British suffered the most damage, with 14 ships and 6,000 lives lost. Germany only lost nine ships and 2,500 men. However, both sides claimed victory as, while the Germans had sunk more ships, the German fleet never again left port for fear of being destroyed. Britain continued to control the North Sea.

> **DID YOU KNOW?**
>
> The commander of the British fleet at Jutland, Admiral Jellicoe, was described as "the only man who could lose the war in an afternoon'.
>
> THINK: what does this mean?

SUBMARINE WARFARE, 1915-18
The use of U-boats posed a serious threat to Britain

What was submarine warfare?
Submarine warfare was conducted by the Germans using U-boats to destroy merchant navy ships.

How many ships did Germany sink using submarine warfare?
U-boats were German submarines which were used to sink enemy ships. In 1915, Germany had 21 U-boats and sank 4% of ships supplying Britain, despite the target being to destroy all merchant shipping. By 1917, the number of German U-boats had increased to 200, and they sank 841,114 tonnes of Allied shipping that year.

What tactics did Germany use in U-boat warfare?
The Germans sank all ships entering British waters, regardless of which country they belonged to, until the sinking of the Lusitania *(p.40)* in 1915 almost brought the USA into the war. This was known as unrestricted U-boat warfare. The policy was abandoned until 1917 when an increasingly desperate Germany tried it again, leading the USA to declare war on Germany.

Why did the Germans use submarine warfare?
U-boats were used to destroy merchant ships bringing in food and war materials from abroad. This was in retaliation for the naval blockade *(p.43)* of German ports by Britain.

How effective was submarine warfare?
Overall, Germany's U-boat campaign did not have the desired effect:
- ✓ Although reduced to six weeks' food supply by 1917, the people of Britain did not starve due to rationing and anti U-boat measures.
- ✓ Likewise, the sinking of American ships brought the USA into the war in April 1917.

> **DID YOU KNOW?**
> The word U-boat comes from the German 'unterseeboot', meaning underwater boat.

ANTI U-BOAT MEASURES
Tackling the U-boat threat

What were anti U-boat measures?
Britain was in danger of losing the war because the shipping which the country relied on was being sunk by German submarines, or U-boats. Countering the U-boat threat was seen as a very important task.

What anti U-boat measures did the British use in the First World War?
There were 4 main anti U-boat measures brought in by the British to try and avoid the damage being done by German U-boats;

- Minefields were laid across the English Channel and in the North Sea. If a U-boat collided with a mine it would be destroyed.
- Depth charges were introduced. These were explosives which were dropped by the British and exploded at certain depths.
- A convoy system was introduced. This meant merchant ships carrying supplies sailed in groups protected by the Royal Navy.
- Q-ships were introduced. These were warships which looked like merchant ships but they were actually armed and could fight the U-boats.

How successful were British anti U-boat measures?

The anti-U-boat measures were extremely successful for a number of reasons:

- Mines were highly effective. In 1917 alone, 20 out of 63 U-boats were sunk after they collided with mines.
- As crews became more experienced with using depth charges, they became more effective. In 1915 only five U-boats were sunk in this way, but the number reached 22 by 1917.
- Convoys were extremely successful, with only 1% of ships in convoy being destroyed.
- Q-ships attacks accounted for 10% of all U-boats sunk.

> **DID YOU KNOW?**
>
> The Royal Navy introduced a newly created convoy system whereby all merchant ships crossing the Atlantic Ocean would travel in groups under the protection of the British navy.

IMPACT OF NAVAL BLOCKADE ON GERMANY
The naval blockade caused severe shortages in Germany for both civilians and the army

What was the naval blockade of Germany?

In 1914, the Royal Navy blockaded German ports. This prevented ships delivering food and vital war supplies to Germany.

What was the impact of the naval blockade of Germany?

The impact of the naval blockade on Germany grew worse as the war progressed and was one of the main reasons for Germany's surrender in 1918. It affected Germany in the following ways:

- Economically: A lack of coal, iron and other raw materials hampered industrial production.
- Socially: Food, fuel and medicine was short. Germany's citizens endured the 'turnip winter' of 1916-17 and hundreds of thousands died from starvation.
- Militarily: A lack of resources meant ammunition and weapons were in short supply by 1918, while troops went hungry. In November, 1918, the navy mutinied.
- Politically: German citizens grew increasingly tired of the war and protests grew. In 1918 there were revolutions in some areas and demands for the abdication of the Kaiser.

> **DID YOU KNOW?**
>
> Germany was so short of cotton by 1918 that some uniforms were made from the fibres of nettles.

THE GALLIPOLI CAMPAIGN
The campaign was an attempt to break the stalemate of the Western Front

❓ What was the Gallipoli campaign?
The campaign was an Allied attempt to open up another campaign and to draw German forces away from the Western front. *(p.31)*

What were the aims of the Gallipoli campaign?
In October 1914, Turkey joined forces with Germany and Austria-Hungary. As Turkey controlled the Dardanelles, which connected the Mediterranean Sea to the Black Sea, Britain could no longer send supplies to Russia, and Russian ships in the Black Sea were trapped. The Gallipoli campaign was needed to:
- ☑ Supply Russia through the Black Sea ports.
- ☑ Break the stalemate on the Western Front by drawing in German forces to support its weaker ally, Turkey.

👤 Who was in charge of the Gallipoli campaign?
It was an Anglo-French operation led by Winston Churchill, the British first lord of the Admiralty.

⏳ When was the Gallipoli campaign?
The campaign ran from February 1915 to January 1916.

📍 Where was the Gallipoli campaign?
At Gallipoli, in northwest Turkey.

What happened during the Gallipoli campaign?
There were a number of events during the Gallipoli campaign:
- ☑ On 19th February, 1915, Anglo-French naval forces began to bombard Turkish positions along the coast. 18th March, 1915 saw the main attack launched, but the fleet retreated after losing three battleships.
- ☑ After the retreat, the decision was taken to launch a ground invasion. Allied troops landed on 25th April, 1915, with the aim of capturing the forts that guarded the entrance to the Dardanelles.
- ☑ The naval attack warned the Turks of the planned invasion, so they were prepared and had strengthened their positions since February 1915.
- ☑ Allied troops landed at Anzac Cove under heavy fire, but established themselves. However, they were unable to move inland and a stalemate developed.
- ☑ The Allies withdrew between 10th December, 1915 and 9th January, 1916. Over 135,000 Allied troops were evacuated. This was the most successful part of the campaign, with only three casualties recorded.

What were the results of the Gallipoli campaign?
There were 5 important consequences of the failed campaign:
- ☑ 204,000 Allied troops were wounded and 48,000 killed.
- ☑ Many soldiers became ill, due to the poor living conditions.
- ☑ The Dardanelles were not captured, and this meant Russia was cut off from Allied support.
- ☑ Germany was able to strengthen its Western Front *(p.31)* position as the Allies looked to make gains in Gallipoli.
- ☑ Churchill and Hamilton (the leaders of the campaign) were removed from their positions.

> **DID YOU KNOW?**
>
> ANZAC stands for Australian and New Zealand Army Corps. Their actions at Gallipoli are commemorated in Australia and New Zealand every year on 25th April.

IMPACT OF RUSSIAN REVOLUTION ON GERMAN STRATEGY
The revolution enabled Germany to focus on the Western Front

What was the Russian surrender in 1917?

In October 1917, Bolsheviks (communists) took control of Russia in a revolution. Their leader, Lenin, pulled Russia out of the First World War. An armistice was agreed in December and a peace treaty was signed in March 1918.

What was the impact of the Russian surrender on the First World War?

There were 3 main consequences of the Russian surrender:
- ☑ It ended the Triple Entente *(p.21)*, weakening the Allied war effort.
- ☑ It allowed the Germans to transfer hundreds of thousands of troops to the Western Front *(p.31)* and launch the Ludendorff Offensive *(p.45)* in spring 1918.
- ☑ The peace treaty of Brest-Litovsk gave Germany vast areas of farmland and raw materials which helped in dealing with shortages caused by the Allied naval blockade. *(p.43)*

> **DID YOU KNOW?**
>
> By March 21st, 1918, Russia's exit had allowed Germany to shift no fewer than 44 divisions of men to the Western Front.

THE LUDENDORFF OFFENSIVE, 1918
Germany's last gamble

What was the Ludendorff Offensive?

The Ludendorff Offensive, also known as the 1918 Spring Offensive or Kaiserschlacht, was a series of German attacks along the Western Front *(p.31)*.

Why was the Ludendorff Offensive launched?

The offensive was launched by Germany for a number of reasons:
- ☑ The USA was sending 50,000 troops each month to the Western Front *(p.31)*, along with vast amounts of weapons and equipment.
- ☑ The withdrawal of Russia freed up hundreds of thousands of troops from the Eastern Front.
- ☑ By 1918 the British naval blockade *(p.43)* meant Germany was running out of food and war materials.

Who planned the Ludendorff Offensive?
Erich Ludendorff, a German general, planned the campaign.

When did the Ludendorff Offensive happen?
The offensive was launched on 21st March 1918 and ended in July 1918.

What happened during the Ludendorff Offensive?
The Ludendorff Offensive was a series of key events:
- On 21st March, 600 German guns began a five-hour bombardment of enemy trenches. This was followed by the release of mustard gas.
- Specially trained and lightly armed stormtroopers then advanced towards the enemy trenches, moving quickly and bypassing strong defences.
- As the British retreated, tens of thousands were captured and the Germans continued to advance.
- 100,000 German infantry soldiers then followed and this strategy allowing the Germans to capture 65km of French territory by July.
- At the Second Battle of the Marne, 20,000 US troops arrived to reinforce the Allies. This halted the German attack.

Why did the Ludendorff Offensive fail?
The offensive failed for a number of reasons:
- Ludendorff sent too many men into France. He did not have any reserves or replacement troops.
- The offensive moved too quickly. The supply chain couldn't keep up and soldiers ran out of food and ammunition.
- The attack created a salient in the German line, which could be attacked from three sides. This meant the Germans were vulnerable to counter-attacks which could break their line.
- Hungry German soldiers stopped to loot food and wine from captured villages and Allied supply dumps, slowing the advance.

> **DID YOU KNOW?**
>
> German commander Erich Ludendorff saw this as a crucial opportunity to launch a new offensive – he hoped to strike a decisive blow to the Allies and convince them to negotiate for peace before fresh troops from the United States could arrive.

THE ENTRY OF THE USA TO THE FIRST WORLD WAR
Here come the Yankees!

What did the USA do when it joined the First World War?
When the USA joined the First World War it reinforced the Allies in Europe, and helped by continuing to supply other allies with food, arms, money, and raw materials.

When did the USA join the First World War?
The USA formally declared war in April 1917.

Why did the USA enter the First World War?

The USA joined the First World War for two key reasons:

- The 'Zimmerman Telegram', from the German foreign secretary to the German ambassador in Mexico, was leaked in January 1917. It offered military and financial support if Mexico agreed to invade the USA. While the Mexicans did not agree, this created tension between Germany and the USA.
- Germany had restarted its unrestricted U-boat campaign. This resulted in the sinking of five American ships in March 1917. As the USA had warned Germany against this after the sinking of the Lusitania (p.40), it felt it had no choice but to declare war on Germany.

When did American troops arrive in Europe after they entered the First World War?

The first American troops landed in Europe in June 1917.

How did America's entry into the First World War help the Allies?

America's entry into the First World War helped in 4 key ways:

- By May 1918 there were over one million US troops in France with tens of thousands arriving each week.
- They enlarged French ports so arriving ships could deliver more men and supplies.
- They built over 1,600km of railway lines to help continue the supply chain.
- They laid over 16,000km of telephone and telegraph cables, to help improve communications between lines.

Why was US entry into the First World War important?

There were a number of significant events in which the USA was involved:

- In the Second Battle of the Marne, two divisions of American soldiers helped to prevent German forces taking Paris during the Ludendorff Offensive (p.45).
- In the Second Battle of Albert, in August 1918, 108,000 US soldiers helped capture 8,000 German soldiers.
- On 12th September 1918, in the Saint-Mihiel Offensive, 500,000 US soldiers attacked the salient created during the Ludendorff Offensive (p.45). Within four days, the salient was under Allied control.
- Between 26th September and 11th November 1918, the US led a combined US-Franco force of more than one million men. Using 300 tanks and 500 US aircraft (p.34), the force advanced 32km towards the German border.
- The US was able to supply the Allies with large numbers of tanks and artillery.

DID YOU KNOW?

Once the Americans had joined the war, they became increasingly paranoid about German influences in the USA!

German names for things like frankfurters, sauerkraut and dachshunds were replaced with 'more American' terms such as liberty sausage, liberty cabbage and liberty hounds.

GENERAL HAIG
The butcher of the Somme?

Who was General Haig?

General Haig was the British commander on the Western Front (p.31) from December 1915. He is a controversial figure as some titled him 'Butcher of the Somme (p.38)', while others believe he was a key factor in winning the war.

What successes did General Haig have?

General Haig had numerous successes during the First World War:

- ✓ Haig relieved the pressure on French forces at Verdun *(p.37)* by starting the Somme *(p.38)* Offensive.
- ✓ The Battle of Passchendaele *(p.39)* succeeded in weakening the German forces.
- ✓ Haig drew German forces away from the Nivelle offensive by leading the Battle of Arras.
- ✓ He masterminded victories at Messines in June 1917.
- ✓ He was willing to be flexible and experiment with the use of tanks, which had success at Cambrai in 1917.
- ✓ He was appointed to win the war for the British, which he ultimately did.

What failures did General Haig have?

Haig had a number of failures during the First World War:

- ✓ His tactic *(p.33)* of attrition resulted in a huge number of casualties, especially at the battles of the Somme *(p.38)* and Passchendaele *(p.39)* .
- ✓ He had a very traditional approach to war, as he was trained as a cavalryman. As such, he was slow to experiment with new methods.
- ✓ By 1917, there was still a stalemate. Haig hadn't masterminded an overall victory despite the huge losses.

DID YOU KNOW?

The first day of the Battle of the Somme, on 1st July, 2016, was disastrous for the British army. In terms of casualties sustained, it suffered the worst day in its history, losing 19,000 men.

FIELD MARSHALL FOCH
The Lion of Verdun

Who was Marshal Ferdinand Foch?

Ferdinand Foch was a French general, prior to and during the First World War. He was promoted to marshall in the summer of 1918.

What was the role of Marshal Ferdinand Foch?

Foch helped stop the German advance at the Battle of the Marne in 1914. During the Ludendorff Offensive *(p.45)* of spring 1918, he became commander-in-chief of all Allied armies on the Western Front *(p.31)*, known as the 'unified command structure'.

What was Marshall Ferdinand Foch's contribution to victory?

Foch planned the Allied 100 Days counter-offensive in 1918 using the latest tactics and technology. In a coordinated attack, the British attacked in the north at the same time as the French and Americans attacked in the south.

> **DID YOU KNOW?**
>
> Petain was a French national hero for his role in the defence of Verdun in the First World War. However, he was later discredited and sentenced to death as head of the French collaborationist government at Vichy in the Second World War.

THE HUNDRED DAYS OFFENSIVE, AUGUST-NOVEMBER 1918
Germany in retreat

What was the 100 Days Offensive?
The 100 Days Offensive was a series of Allied attacks which ended the First World War.

What happened during the 100 Days Offensive?
There were 2 key events of the 100 Days Offensive:
- At Amiens an artillery attack and creeping barrage broke through the German lines and allowed an Allied advance of 25km. Allied troops also captured 48,000 German soldiers.
- After breaking the front line at Amiens, the Allies forced the Germans back to the Hindenburg Line which was broken by 8th October. At this point, the Germans were now in all-out retreat.

When was the 100 Days Offensive?
The offensive began with the Battle of Amiens on 8th August 1918, and ended officially on 11th November 1918 when Germany signed the Armistice.

Why was the 100 Days Offensive important?
The 100 Days Offensive was important for 2 key reasons:
- It allowed the Allies to break the Hindenburg Line, a defensive line of three trench systems. Once this was broken, the Germans retreated in huge numbers.
- The offensive led to the German High Command seeking an armistice which came into effect on 11th November, 1918.

> **DID YOU KNOW?**
>
> **The Hundred Days Offensive didn't actually last for 100 days.**
> It only lasted 95 days from 8th August 1918 to 11th November 1918.

THE END OF THE FIRST WORLD WAR
Armistice and defeat

Was Germany defeated in the First World War?
Germany requested an armistice, and this was signed between Germany and the Allies on 11th November 1918. This was the formal end to the fighting while a peace treaty was negotiated.

What were the reasons for the German defeat in the First World War?
There were a number of reasons for Germany's overall defeat in the First World War:

- ☑ Food and famine. Germany's agricultural production was poor and it relied on foreign imports. However, the British naval blockade *(p.43)* starved Germany of these, and there was a series of bad harvests. As the Germans starved, they rioted against the government.
- ☑ Political turmoil. There was a series of riots and revolts against the government. In October there was a naval mutiny, followed by revolutions in Munich and, finally, riots in Berlin. This caused the kaiser to abdicate.
- ☑ Military defeat. Germany realised it was facing a military defeat. With the failure of the Ludendorff Offensive *(p.45)*, the introduction of two million US troops and its allies surrendering, Germany knew it could no longer continue the fight.

> **DID YOU KNOW?**
>
> The armistice was signed in a railway carriage in Compiegne, France. Hitler used the same railway carriage to accept the French surrender in 1940.

GLOSSARY

A

Abdicate - to give up a position of power or a responsibility.

Alliance - a union between groups or countries that benefits each member.

Allies - parties working together for a common objective, such as countries involved in a war. In both world wars, 'Allies' refers to those countries on the side of Great Britain.

Ammunition - collective term given to bullets and shells.

Annex, Annexation, Annexed - to forcibly acquire territory and add it to a larger country.

Armistice - an agreement between two or more opposing sides in a war to stop fighting.

Artillery - large guns used in warfare.

Assassinate - to murder someone, usually an important figure, often for religious or political reasons.

Assassination - the act of murdering someone, usually an important person.

Attrition - the act of wearing down an enemy until they collapse through continued attacks.

Autocrat - a ruler who has absolute power over their country.

B

Blockade - a way of blocking or sealing an area to prevent goods, supplies or people from entering or leaving. It often refers to blocking transport routes.

Box barrage - The firing shells at the enemy on three sides to prevent them retreating or sending reinforcements into a battle.

C

Campaign - a political movement to get something changed; in military terms, it refers to a series of operations to achieve a goal.

Casualties - people who have been injured or killed, such as during a war, accident or catastrophe.

Cavalry - the name given to soldiers who fight on horseback.

Central Powers - Germany and its allies during the First World War.

Civilian - a non-military person.

Colonies, Colony - a country or area controlled by another country and occupied by settlers.

Convoy - a group of ships or vehicles travelling together, usually protected by armed troops.

Counter-attack - an attack made in response to one by an opponent.

Creeping barrage - a slowly advancing artillery bombardment which attacking troops can follow for protection.

D

Deadlock - a situation where no action can be taken and neither side can make progress against the other; effectively a draw.

Dreadnought - A battleship, which was more powerful in firepower and defence than prior models.

Dud - a bomb, shell or mine that fails to explode.

E

Economic - relating to the economy; also used when justifying something in terms of profitability.

Economy - a country, state or region's position in terms of production and consumption of goods and services, and the supply of money.

Empire - a group of states or countries ruled over and controlled by a single monarch.

Encircle, Encirclement - a military term for enemy forces isolating and surrounding their target.

F

Famine - a severe food shortage resulting in starvation and death, usually the result of bad harvests.

Foreign policy - a government's strategy for dealing with other nations.

Front - in war, the area where fighting is taking place.

H

Heir - someone who is entitled to property or rank following the current owner or holder's death.

I

Imperial, Imperialisation, Imperialism, Imperialist - is the practice or policy of taking possession of, and extending political and economic control over other areas or territories. Imperialism always requires the use of military, political or economic power by a stronger nation over that of a weaker one. An imperialist is someone who supports or practices imperialism and imperial relates to a system of empire, for example the British Empire.

Import - to bring goods or services into a different country to sell.

Independence, Independent - to be free of control, often meaning by another country, allowing the people of a nation the ability to govern themselves.

Industrialisation, Industrialise, Industrialised - the process of developing industry in a country or region where previously there was little or none.

Infantry - soldiers who march and fight on foot.

K

Kaiser - the German word for a king or emperor.

GLOSSARY

L

Lord, Lords - a man of high status, wealth and authority.

M

Mandate - authority to carry out a policy.

Merchant ships - unarmed ships used for carrying supplies and goods.

Mine - an explosive device usually hidden underground or underwater.

Minister - a senior member of government, usually responsible for a particular area such as education or finance.

Mobilisation - the action of a country getting ready for war by preparing and organising its armed forces.

Morass - an area of swampy or very wet and muddy ground which is difficult to cross.

Mutiny - a rebellion or revolt, in particular by soldiers or sailors against their commanding officers.

N

Nationalism, Nationalist, Nationalistic - identifying with your own nation and supporting its interests, often to the detriment or exclusion of other nations.

Naval supremacy - when a navy is that strong, enemies are unable to attack; sometimes referred to as command of the sea.

No man's land - the land between the opposing sides' trenches in the First World War.

O

Offensive - another way of saying an attack or campaign.

P

Province, Provinces - part of an empire or a country denoting areas that have been divided for administrative purposes.

Psychological - referring to a person's mental or emotional state.

Q

Quagmire - an area of swampy or very wet and muddy ground which is difficult to cross.

R

Rationing - limiting goods that are in high demand and short supply.

Rebels - people who rise in opposition or armed resistance against an established government or leader.

Reconnaissance - observation of an enemy in order to gain useful information such as its position, strategy or capabilities.

Revolution - the forced overthrow of a government or social system by its own people.

Riots - violent disturbances involving a crowd of people.

Rolling barrage - a slowly advancing artillery bombardment which attacking troops can follow for protection.

S

Sabotage - to deliberately destroy, damage or obstruct, especially to gain a political or military advantage.

Salient - in military terms, a piece of land that protrudes into enemy territory; also known as a bulge.

Slavic people, Slavs - the main ethnic group of people living in Eastern Europe.

Splendid isolation - a British foreign policy in the 19th century which aimed to focus on the British Empire and keep Britain out of European wars.

Stalemate - a situation where no action can be taken and neither side can make progress against the other; effectively a draw.

Strategy - a plan of action outlining how a goal will be achieved.

T

Tactic - a strategy or method of achieving a goal.

Territories, Territory - an area of land under the control of a ruler/country.

Treaty - a formal agreement, signed and ratified by two or more parties.

U

U-boat - the German name for a submarine.

Ultimatum - a final demand, with the threat of consequences if it is not met.

W

Weltpolitik - Germany's pre-First World War foreign policy which aimed to turn Germany into a global power by acquiring overseas colonies and developing its navy.

INDEX

A
Aircraft - 34
Alliances - 15
Allied 100 Days - 49
Anti U-boat measures - 42
Arms Race - 22
Artillery - 37
Assassination, Archduke Franz Ferdinand - 28
Austria-Hungary before 1914 - 20

B
Balkan War, First - 26
Balkan War, Second - 27
Battle of Jutland - 41
Battle of Passchendaele - 39
Battle of Verdun - 37
Battle of the Somme - 38
Black Hand - 27
Blockade - 43
Bosnian Crisis - 25
Britain before 1914 - 17
Britain, entry to WW1 - 30

D
Deadlock, Western Front - 32
Dreadnought - 23

F
Ferdinand Foch - 48
First Balkan War - 26
First Moroccan Crisis - 23
First World War - 14
Foch, Ferdinand - 48
France before 1914 - 18
Franz Ferdinand, assassination - 28

G
Gallipoli campaign - 44
Germany before 1914 - 19
Germany, defeat - 50
Great Powers - 16

H
Haig, General Douglas - 47

I
Imperialism - 15

J
July Days (July Crisis), 1914 - 29
Jutland, Battle of - 41

K
Kaiserschlacht - 45

L
Ludendorff Offensive - 45
Lusitania, sinking of - 40

M
Machine guns - 34
Militarism - 14
Moroccan Crisis, 1905 - 23
Moroccan Crisis, 1911 - 24

N
Nationalism - 16
Naval Race - 23

O
One Hundred Day Offensive - 49

P
Passchendaele, Battle of - 39
Poison gas - 35

R
Rearmament - 22
Russia in 1914 - 19
Russia, withdrawal from war - 45

S
Schlieffen Plan - 30
Second Balkan War - 27
Second Moroccan Crisis - 24
Somme, Battle of - 38
Spring Offensive - 45

INDEX

Stalemate, Western Front - *32*

Submarine warfare - *42*

T

Tactics - *33*

Tanks - *36*

Trench system - *32*

Triple Alliance - *21*

Triple Entente - *21*

U

U-boat warfare - *42*

USA, entry to WWI - *46*

V

Verdun, Battle of - *37*

W

Weapons
    Aircraft - *34*
    Artillery - *37*
    Machine guns - *34*
    Poison gas - *35*
    Tanks - *36*

Western Front - *31*

Western Front, deadlock - *32*

www.ingramcontent.com/pod-product-compliance
Lightning Source LLC
Chambersburg PA
CBHW050718090526
44588CB00014B/2337